BE A WASTE WARRIOR!

TRAVEL WARRIOR

GOING GREEN

T0025371

by Claudia Martin
Consultant: David Hawksett, BSc

BEARPORT
PUBLISHING

Minneapolis, Minnesota

Credits: cover, © Inna Reznik/Shutterstock; 1, © Huang Jenhung/Shutterstock; 4, © MikeDotta/ Shutterstock; 4–5b, © Muratart/Shutterstock; 5r, © Dbtrotman/Shutterstock; 6, © Mdbildes/ Shutterstock; 7, © Anele Nova/Shutterstock; 7b, © Africa Studio/Shutterstock; 8, © Wk1003mike/ Shutterstock; 8–9b, © PR Image Factory/Shutterstock; 10, © Wavebreakmedia/Shutterstock; 11, © Salena Stinchcombe/Shutterstock; 12, © Lazyllama/Shutterstock; 13, © Darren Baker/Shutterstock; 14, © Just dance/Shutterstock; 15, © Myboys.me/Shutterstock; 16–17b, © Kajornyot Wildlife Photography/ Shutterstock; 17t, © Frantic00/Shutterstock; 18–19b, © Fuss Sergey/Shutterstock; 19t, © Dmegias/ Shutterstock; 20, © Michaeljung/Shutterstock; 21, © Anna Moskvina/Shutterstock; 22, © Monkey Business Images/Shutterstock; 23, © Prostock–studio/Shutterstock; 24, © Egd/Shutterstock; 25, © Ocollins/Shutterstock; 26–27b, © CGN089/Shutterstock; 27, © Africa Studio/Shutterstock.

Editor: Sarah Eason
Proofreader: Jennifer Sanderson
Designer: Paul Myerscough
Illustrator: Jessica Moon
Picture Researcher: Rachel Blount

Library of Congress Cataloging-in-Publication Data

Names: Martin, Claudia, author.
Title: Travel warrior : going green / by Claudia Martin.
Description: Minneapolis, Minnesota : Bearport Publishing Company, 2021. |
   Series: Be a waste warrior! | Includes bibliographical references and
   index.
Identifiers: LCCN 2020030834 (print) | LCCN 2020030835 (ebook) | ISBN
   9781647476991 (library binding) | ISBN 9781647477066 (paperback) | ISBN
   9781647477134 (ebook)
Subjects: LCSH: Travel—Environmental aspects—Juvenile literature. |
   Transportation—Waste minimization—Juvenile literature. | Source
   reduction (Waste management)—Juvenile literature. | Environmental
   protection—Citizen participation—Juvenile literature.
Classification: LCC G156.5.E58 M36 2021 (print) | LCC G156.5.E58 (ebook)
   | DDC 363.73/7—dc23
LC record available at https://lccn.loc.gov/2020030834
LC ebook record available at https://lccn.loc.gov/2020030835

For more information, write to Bearport Publishing, 5357 Penn Avenue South, Minneapolis, MN 55419. Printed in the United States of America.

CONTENTS

THE BATTLE TO SAVE EARTH!

We look forward to vacations for months and enjoy the memories for many years afterward. But waste created by everything from resorts to transportation is a global problem. Even while you're traveling, you can do your part in the battle against waste. Be a waste warrior on the go!

The Three Problems with Waste

Heaps of Garbage Much of our garbage—including trash from planes, trains, and hotels—is thrown into **landfills**. But when waste breaks down in landfills, it can harm our environment. **Plastic** can leak harmful things into the soil and air. Waste in landfills lets off methane gas as it breaks down. On top of that, the waste in landfills just sits there—stored up for a future generation to deal with. That is why waste warriors avoid creating waste!

We have created landfills to deal with our huge amounts of waste.

Wasted Resources When we travel by bus, train, boat, or plane, **oil** is burned to power the vehicle. Oil is a **natural resource** of which we have a limited supply. It is a **fossil fuel** that takes millions of years to form from the remains of dead animals and plants—but it burns in just a few seconds.

Polluted Planet Burning gasoline in the engines of airplanes and cars also creates air **pollution**. Fossil fuels, such as gasoline, release **carbon dioxide** and other gases when burned. These gases trap the sun's heat around Earth, causing temperatures to rise and changing the world's weather over time—this is called **climate change**.

Our world is filled with trash from travelers.

Carbon dioxide released by airplanes worsens climate change.

5

The Six Rs

Have a trip planned? Want to be a waste warrior while you have fun? Here are six tools you can use to help with the war on waste. Remember that every positive step, however tiny, helps us all travel in the right direction.

Refuse If you have a choice, say no thanks to keepsakes that will wind up in the garbage a year down the road.

Reduce Try to reduce air pollution by using public transportation, which uses up less oil than everyone going individually.

Reuse Pour the shampoo and other liquids you will need into reusable bottles instead of buying travel-sized bottles.

Repair Repair suitcases and other travel equipment when it breaks, rather than tossing it out and buying something new.

Recycle Aim to **recycle** all the metal, glass, plastic, and paper you go through while traveling, so it can be made into something new.

Rot Unwanted foods can go in a **compost** bin to rot away. Try to find a way to compost on the road!

Try sharing shampoos and shower gels with family or friends while you are away.

Keepsakes often end up in the trash.

Repairing a suitcase might save you money and fight the planet's waste problem at the same time!

PACK A SNACK

Who doesn't get hungry when they're traveling? That bag of trail mix or fruit snacks looks good, but it might not be so good for the environment. Food packaging can be a waste problem when you're at home, but it's even more of an issue when you're traveling.

Many of the snacks sold in gas stations, rest stops, and airports are in single-serving-size packaging, which creates more waste than bulk packaging. Packaging makes up more than one-fifth of all the waste in landfills. On top of that, making packaging often uses up our natural resources, including wood, water, metal, and oil. But a waste warrior can find a simple solution!

Any plastic packaging that we throw away while traveling becomes a landfill problem.

What a Waste!

Every year, more than 32 million tons (29 million MT) of packaging waste is dumped into U.S. landfills. That's the weight of about 16 million cars!

When traveling, it can be hard to find a snack that is healthy for ourselves and the environment!

Ready to battle snack packaging waste? Before you leave for your trip, pack snacks from home. Pour snack foods into single-serving reusable containers. Even better, pack a snack that needs no container, such as an apple. If you plan ahead, when you get hungry, you'll have a snack that won't make trash. It's a tasty and eco-friendly way to be a waste warrior!

Warriors Can Try:

You don't need to buy boxes or bags for single-serving snack packs. Instead, think about any packaging in your recycling pile that could be reused.

- Cookie or chocolate boxes
- Fruit or veggie baskets and bags
- Cardboard pasta or snack-food boxes
- Old bread bags

Make sandwiches for the whole family before you leave home. Then wrap them in a bread bag to go.

Fill a reusable, washable container with healthy trail mix and slip it into your backpack. It will keep your energy levels high as you trek, cycle, or fly!

TAKE A DRINK

You're bound to get thirsty while you're traveling. But think carefully before buying a bottle of water or soda. It only takes minutes to drink, but the bottle could last for hundreds of years.

Plastic bottles are usually made of **polyethylene terephthalate (PET)**. PET is a problem because it does not break down quickly. Natural materials, such as food, rot away quickly in a process called **biodegrading**. But bottles made from PET could take around 500 years to break down. And as they break down, harmful chemicals can leak into the environment. But there is good news—no waste warrior needs to go thirsty!

Plastic bottles can wind up in the ocean if they are left by wasteful travelers.

What a Waste!

Around the globe, one million plastic bottles are bought every minute— and that number is always going up.

Plastic harms the environment, and it may harm our bodies, too. Studies have shown that plastic from water bottles can leak into the water, which could cause long-term health issues.

What can a waste warrior do to reduce plastic bottle waste? Simple! Get a reusable bottle that will last for many years. You can use it at home and when you travel. If you do end up buying a plastic bottle when you're traveling, try reusing it. Drink up. Then, wash it and refill it as you go. When the bottle gets too old to reuse, throw it in the recycling.

Warriors Can Try:

You would be amazed by what PET bottles can turn into!

- Fabrics used in athletic clothes and shoes
- Plastic pens
- Warm, fluffy filling for jackets and sleeping bags
- Packaging tape
- Furniture and building materials

Maybe your sweater used to be a bottle!

PASSPORT
W

Although a reusable water bottle is more expensive than a single-use one, it will save you money in the long term.

FIND A FORK

When we're on the move, we often buy meals to eat as we go. And that food often comes with plastic spoons, knives, and forks to eat with. These are single-use plastics—they are intended to be used just once and then tossed. Single-use plastics are one of the world's biggest waste problems. Not only do they pile up in landfills, but making them creates pollution.

Most plastics are made from oil or **natural gas**. These fossil fuels need to be drilled from deep in the ground. This releases carbon dioxide into the air, worsening climate change. And when oil is transported from drilling sites to factories, it can leak from pipes and ships, polluting oceans. Waste warriors can solve this problem one fork at a time!

In 2013, workers hurried to clean up oil from a beach in the Gulf of Thailand after an oil pipe leaked in the water.

Plastic forks are usually made out of polypropylene or polystyrene, which both come from fossil fuels.

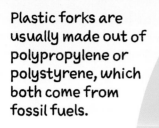

What a Waste!

Around 40 billion single-use plastic utensils are thrown away every year in the United States.

A waste warrior can say "No, thank you" to plastic forks, spoons, and knives. When traveling, carry your own reusable utensils (but be careful about where you bring reusable knives). If you forget to bring your own fork and spoon, accept plastic freebies and then wash them when you get home or to your hotel. If you are careful with single-use plastics, they are not so single-use after all!

Warriors Can Try:

Sometimes restaurants offer single-use utensils that are not made of plastic. Keep an eye out for these materials.

- Wood
- **Bamboo**
- **Bioplastics**, which are usually made from plants
- Foods, such as rice and flour!

An all-purpose utensil made from recycled plastic is a perfect addition to your travel bag.

Wooden utensils are a traveling waste warrior's best friend.

FORGET YOUR TICKET

Got your bag? Check! Packed a snack? Check! Got your ticket? Hold on, Waste Warrior. If your ticket is printed on paper, then it poses a waste problem. As paper piles up, it threatens our planet.

Around the world, about 15 billion trees are cut down every year. Some are used to make paper. Even paper that comes from managed forests, where new trees are planted to replace those cut down, isn't perfect. Cutting down trees, replanting trees, and making paper uses fossil fuels to power machines and vehicles. Water is used in every stage of paper production, wasting an important natural resource. So perhaps it's time to forget paper tickets altogether, Waste Warrior!

When traveling, it can be difficult to find a recycling bin, so many paper tickets will end up in a landfill.

One-third of paper produced in the United States comes from freshly cut trees.

What a Waste!

Around one billion trees' worth of paper is thrown away each year in the United States.

There might be an easy way to reduce ticket waste. Your grown-up can probably download a **digital** version of your ticket and show it on-screen. If it's not possible for you to go digital, hold on to your paper ticket until you find a recycling bin. While you're on the journey, use the back of your ticket for drawing, playing games, or writing a letter—the old-fashioned way!

Warriors Can Try:

You might be surprised by how much paper you could collect when you're traveling. Often, there are ways to go without these common paper items.

- Look for a digital option or posted signs instead of taking paper maps.

- Take a photo of flyers for attractions instead of grabbing a copy.

- Look for bus, train, and subway schedules posted online or in a public space rather than taking paper.

Scanning an e-ticket is the eco-friendly way to travel!

Finding your way is easier with an online map than with an easily torn paper map.

18:54

Restaurants

Search

1 **Balade Restaurant** 150 ★★★★★
Main Street, 61

2 **East Village Bistro** 220 ★★★★★
Broad Street, 164

3 **Joe Cof** 350 ★★★★★
Chestnut S

4 **Steakhou**

FIND OUT ABOUT FUEL

Whether you're setting off by car, bus, train, boat, or plane, it's time to talk **carbon footprints**. The amount of carbon dioxide an activity releases is called a carbon footprint. And transportation has a very high carbon footprint. The **fuel** burned by vehicle engines accounts for one-quarter of all the carbon released in the United States.

Human activities have released so much carbon dioxide over the last century that the Earth's atmosphere is now trapping more heat from the sun. As a result, Earth's air and oceans have already increased in temperature by 2 degrees Fahrenheit (1 degree Celsius). This doesn't sound like a lot, but those extra couple of degrees are reducing snow cover and sea ice, causing more floods and storms than before and changing habitats for plants and animals. So what can a waste warrior do?

Cars release heat-trapping carbon dioxide through their tailpipes.

What a Waste!

The average gasoline-powered car releases 0.79 pounds (0.36 kg) of carbon dioxide every mile (1.6 km).

Rongbuk Glacier in the Himalaya Mountains is shrinking fast as temperatures rise.

The easiest way to reduce your transportation carbon footprint is to make some footprints of your own. When your journey is short enough, walk it! Or think about riding your bike. For longer journeys, taking public transportation is also a good option, since everyone on the bus or train can share the carbon footprint of the journey. When driving is the only option, consider carpooling. By sharing with friends and family, you will reduce the number of vehicles burning fuel as they make the same journey.

Warriors Can Try:

When flying is your only option, there are still ways to reduce your carbon footprint as you take to the skies.

- Packing lightly adds less weight to the plane. Heavier planes burn more fuel.

- If it is not too expensive, try to take a direct flight. Planes burn a lot of fuel during takeoffs and landings.

- Grow your own plants. Plants absorb carbon dioxide from the air so you will be doing one more thing to help reduce carbon in the air.

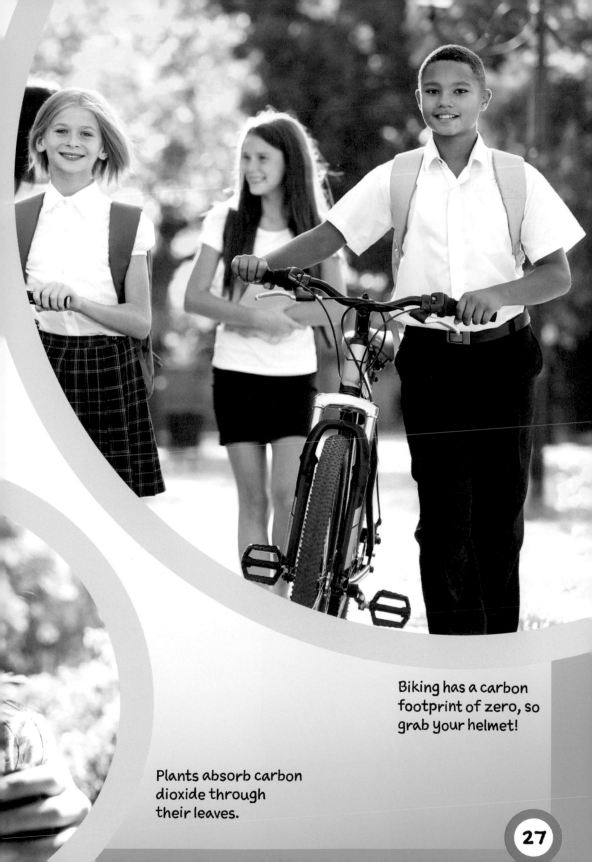

Biking has a carbon footprint of zero, so grab your helmet!

Plants absorb carbon dioxide through their leaves.

Organize a Beach Cleanup

Everyone loves to visit the beach for a vacation getaway. But it's not so fun if the beach is littered with trash. What can a waste warrior do? Gather some friends, roll up your sleeves, and clean up!

You will need:

- Thick work or gardening gloves
- Sunscreen, sun hats, and closed-toe shoes
- Reusable bottles with drinking water
- Trash bags
- Hand sanitizer
- Something that can play music
- A camera or phone that can take pictures

1 Choose a beach (or a local park) near you that needs a cleanup. Make sure your spot is safely away from busy roads or dangerous cliffs.

2 With an adult's help, find out if you will need permission for your cleanup. A call to the local parks department is a good place to start.

3 Gather the supplies you need. You could ask a local hardware or grocery store if they might donate any items for your cleanup.

BEACH

4 With an adult's help, contact local recycling companies and your community's solid waste department to arrange where you will drop off any garbage, glass, metal, paper, or plastic items you find.

5 Pick a time for your cleanup when you think most people might be free. Ask friends, family, and neighbors to volunteer. Make sure you get some help from adults who can handle dangerous items, such as broken or sharp objects.

6 Get going on your beach cleanup! All your volunteers should wear thick gloves, wear sunscreen, drink plenty of water, and wash up when they are done. Listening to music while cleaning will help make it fun for everyone.

7 Take photos of the waste you collect and see if you can post them at the beach to raise awareness.

Glossary

bamboo a quickly growing, tall grass with a woody stem

biodegrading the breaking down of waste by living things, such as bacteria and fungi

bioplastics plastics made from living things, such as plants, rather than from fossil fuels

carbon dioxide an invisible gas in the air that is released when fossil fuels are burned

carbon footprints measures of the amount of carbon dioxide released into the atmosphere as a result of the activities of a particular individual, organization, or community

climate change the change of Earth's climate and weather patterns, including the warming of Earth's air and oceans, due to human activities

compost rotted plants and food that can be used to feed soil

digital information that is sent and stored by a computer or other electronic equipment

fossil fuel a fuel made from the remains of animals and plants that lived long ago

fuel a material that can be burned to make heat or power machines

landfills pits where waste is dumped and then covered by soil

natural gas a gas that is found underground and can be burned to make heat or power

natural resource a useful material found in nature, such as a tree, water, metals, and oil

oil also called petroleum; a liquid fuel found in the ground that is made from the remains of dead animals and plants

plastic a machine-made material, usually made from oil, that can be shaped when soft, then sets to be hard or flexible

pollution any harmful material that is put into the ground, air, or water

polyethylene terephthalate (PET) a plastic that is often used to make bottles

recycle to collect, sort, and treat waste so it is turned into materials that can be used again

Read More

Andrus, Aubre. *101 Small Ways to Change the World.* Oakland, CA: Lonely Planet Kids, 2018.

Beer, Julie. *Kids vs. Plastic: Ditch the Straw and Find the Pollution Solution to Bottles, Bags, and Other Single-Use Plastics.* Washington, D.C.: National Geographic Kids, 2020.

Dickmann, Nancy. *The Impact of Energy (Impact on Earth).* New York: Crabtree Publishing Company, 2020.

Martin, Claudia. *Clothing Warrior: Going Green (Be a Waste Warrior!).* Minneapolis: Bearport, 2021.

Learn More Online

1. Go to **www.factsurfer.com**
2. Enter "**Travel Warrior**" into the search box.
3. Click on the cover of this book to see a list of websites.

Index